"Rhonda Brown has eyes to see the beauty of God's world despite its brokenness. Coupled with that, she stewards the keen gift of captivating my imagination despite using only a few words with each composition. If you are not yet into poetry, start here. If you love poetry, read this book and be blessed."

Dr. Gary G. Hoag - President & CEO (Global Trust Partners), author of numerous books, and (most importantly) fellow Christ-follower

✳

Take an hour and settle into your favorite chair.
Reading Rhonda Brown's poems is sure to transport you to another realm where what is rarely seen, though perhaps vaguely sensed is verbalized in the beauty of her stunning poetry. The under-appreciated desert habitat comes alive in her word pictures. Each poem deepens one's admiration and wonder at the desert and her craftsmanship. From there one is ushered into secret rooms of praise that are anything but shallow. Colorful. Heartfelt. Deep. Personal. Beautiful.

Crystal Knapp
Founder, Reach UP Magazine
Filling the void in print and digital communication for and by marginalized women.

Authors often see common objects and situations from a different perspective. I love to observe nature as I travel, and often write about what the Lord shows me.

So I'm fascinated by watching Rhonda Brown share her observations of nature, weaving them with Scripture and perception into poems of beauty and depth.

I come away from one of her poems with new insights and thoughts, and I'm eager to have this volume on my shelf.

Elsi Dodge
author, *RV Tourist: Hacks for the Highway*

I Weave a Song of Praise

A Collection of Poems
by Rhonda Brown

WESTBOW
PRESS®
A DIVISION OF THOMAS NELSON
& ZONDERVAN

WestBow Press books may be ordered through booksellers or by contacting:

WestBow Press
A Division of Thomas Nelson & Zondervan
1663 Liberty Drive
Bloomington, IN 47403
www.westbowpress.com
844-714-3454

Because of the dynamic nature of the Internet, any web addresses or links contained in this book may have changed since publication and may no longer be valid. The views expressed in this work are solely those of the author and do not necessarily reflect the views of the publisher, and the publisher hereby disclaims any responsibility for them.

Design Credits:
Graphic and Cover Design: John Tarr
Cover photo: palo verde tree in bloom.
Psalms 56:8 stamp collage stamped by Rhonda Brown. Glass canning bottle:
©Good Stamps*Stamp Goods, artist Carole Finley, used by permission.
Madonna Image: Post Modern Design. Used by permission.
Pear hand-carved image ©A Stamp in the Hand Co. Artist: Sue Nan Douglass.
Used by permission. Stamped with watercolor markers by Rhonda Brown

All Scripture quotations, unless otherwise indicated, are taken from the Holy Bible, New International Version®, NIV®. Copyright ©1973, 1978, 1984, 2011 by Biblica, Inc.® Used by permission of Zondervan. All rights reserved worldwide. www.zondervan.com The "NIV" and "New International Version" are trademarks registered in the United States Patent and Trademark Office by Biblica, Inc.®

Scripture quotations marked (RSV) are from Revised Standard Version of the Bible, copyright © 1946, 1952, and 1971 National Council of the Churches of Christ in the United States of America. Used by permission. All rights reserved worldwide.

Scripture quotations marked (NLT) are taken from the Holy Bible, New Living Translation, copyright ©1996, 2004, 2015 by Tyndale House Foundation. Used by permission of Tyndale House Publishers, Carol Stream, Illinois 60188. All rights reserved.

ISBN: 978-1-6642-4402-3 (sc)
ISBN: 978-1-6642-4403-0 (e)

Library of Congress Control Number: 2021918194

Print information available on the last page.

WestBow Press rev. date: 10/26/2021

Contents

A Letter to My Readers,

I've batted around what this portion of my book ought to be called: *Acknowledgements? Preface?* I pondered what I wanted to say to my readers and drafted multiple pieces trying to articulate my thoughts. I finally decided that I wanted to begin with, simply, a letter to my readers.

I expect that many of my readers will be friends who already know me and are well-acquainted with where I'm coming from. I hope that eventually there will be others beyond that circle, and I'd like to tell them something about how these poems came to be.

I was in mid-life before I began to seriously write poetry, and it was a long time before poetry gained any real priority in my life. I was busy with other things. Over the years, however, it has become more and more natural to express in poems those things that are most important to me.

Most of the poems in this book relate to what I regard as the most important element in my life: that I am a Christian. I am convinced that the Christian faith is true, and that the Bible is a trustworthy document, revealing to us a Creator and Redeemer who is powerful, creative, and loving. What I write springs from that conviction.

My writing also springs from my physical surroundings. I live in a desert area of God's creation, and the beauties of this particular locale also find a place in my poems. I love soaking it up, trying to capture in words what I see around me.

As time has passed, my little portfolio of poems has expanded, and in the last several years I began to contemplate the possibility of creating my own book. That grew from wishful thinking to genuine intention, but all the unknowns of the process were quite mysterious and daunting. Fortunately, being a member of the Arizona State Poetry Society put me in contact with a number of people for whom the process was neither mysterious nor as daunting, and they have been generous in sharing their skills and knowledge. In the preparation of the book, I have received wonderful gifts from some very kind friends.

Fellow poet Carol Hogan has gifted me with her knowledge and experience in readying a book for publication, and with warm encouragement every step of the way.

John Tarr, fellow participant with us in the Phoenix chapter of Reasons to Believe, has done the graphic design for the book, setting up illustrations and designing the cover, and creating my website at poetmonk.com.

I am also indebted to the artists who gave me permission to use their images in the book. Thanks to Kathie Okamoto of A Stamp in the Hand and artist Sue Nan Douglass for permission to use their hand carved pear image; to Emmy Good of Good Stamps*Stamp Goods for the use of the canning jar image created by Carole Finley; and to Kathy Martin of Postmodern Design for the use of their Madonna image.

My long-time friend and fellow wordsmith, Elsi Dodge, has been a sounding board on many issues, ranging from proper Bible citation to punctuation. We agreed that I did not have to be consistent from poem to poem, and I have happily pursued my practice of using standard punctuation when I felt that it served the poem well, and following it more loosely when the meaning was clear without it. Some of you who are especially attentive to details may find that helpful to know.

Two communities of which I am a part have stood behind me with steady encouragement. Friends in Arizona State Poetry Society— both in Mustang Poets and East Valley Poets—have been the first to hear many of these poems and have provided gentle critiquing. Fellow Jesus-followers, both from my church and from parachurch groups in which we volunteer, have supported me in prayer for the completion of the book and for its appearance at the proper time, for the glory of God.

To all of these helping hands, many, many thanks.

To all of you who will be reading who already know Jesus, may these words bless and nourish your hearts. If you don't know him yet, may they pique your curiosity and nudge you to deeper investigation.

In our good Lord,
Rhonda Brown

p.s. I didn't want to clutter up a book of poems with footnotes. The few spots where I felt they might be helpful have been identified with an asterisk, and the explanation provided in a brief page of notes at the end of the book. I think the information provided there is adequate.

Dedicated to the memory of

Guy Poppy

and

Marie Poppy

whose thoughtful reading
and encouragement
nourished my heart

Desert Hymn

Earth with her thousand voices praises God.
— *S.T. Coleridge* *

God's passion poured
on desert dwellers
shouts out
in dove wing and tortoise shell,
in cardinal red
and yellow cactus flower.
Grackles' black elegance
and lizards' varicolored beading
spring alike from the Creator's mind.

Saguaro arms lift high in praise;
orange-flagged ocotillo trembles
and yucca's creamy candles
blaze with waxen unburning.
Incense of creosote,
mesquite and purple sage
release aroma of thanksgiving.

Hummingbirds flit,
finding nurture in sweet to sweet.
Bees swim
in fairy-duster pools
brimming with pollen,
giving praise to the God of their provision.

Oh, thousand desert voices,
shout, shout praise
for this passion poured!

Palo Verde

Evanescence tethered
gossamer contained—
not given leave to soar
it strains at root and soil

And its gold sinks
sheds its wealth of blossom
into yellow drift
pooling and lapping
at the foot of the smooth green bark

Earthbound ethereal
here you lay your carpet of bloom
on the desert floor
at my feet.

Color Song

Color clambers everywhere—
Oleander cascades over stuccoed walls,
white to pink to deeper pink,
brilliant chorus of color.
Bougainvillea scales trellises,
glowing as if from light within.

Jacarandas bloom ethereal in purple;
Palo Verde dances gold-clad,
and everywhere green,
dusty or fresh,
climbs into my eyes and sings,
clamoring, "See!" and "Hear!"

Miniatures

What loveliness is packed
In tiny things—

Scaled wings and feathered wings
All golds and teals
Emeralds and rubies

Buzzing flight
And noiseless creeping
Shrill chorus
Or single melodic song

Beetle's ebon shell
Dragonfly's iridescence
Hummingbird's gleaming blur

Short fragile lives
Lavished with glory—

What loveliness is packed
In tiny things.

Ornament

This jeweled day
sun-shot with brilliance of bougainvillea
and green-glistening from peridot to emerald—

a hawk slices amber across the sky
and hummingbirds flash
iridescent arcs on azure.

May I wear about my throat
this jeweled day.

I Weave a Song
of Praise

I weave a song of praise to you,
Creator God,
who spoke the atoms into orbit
spread out the heavens in vast expanse
gathered planets' mass
set the sun alight
and spun the earth in place
then shaped with molten lava
with limestone sediment and tilted strata

Who scattered cirrus and cumulus
gave DNA its complex shape
set birds in flight
and fish to swimming
fashioned skin and bone
feather, fin
golden fur of tamarin
sleek orca's hide
made man from dust
and stamped your image there

Thee I adore,
Creator God,
who built this habitation with such love
watched it fall
then bought it back with blood

I weave a song of praise to you,
Creator God,
who will build anew
in perfection
and dwell with those who trust you
all danger gone
pain banished
no end to life
with you,
with you.

God So Loved

An Elaboration on John 3:16

For God so loved the world—
> So loved this blue-green jewel
> Floating in perfect orbit
> In the vast reach of space
>
> With its myriad inhabitants
> The earth and its creatures
> And man in God's own image
> Those sheep without a shepherd

That he gave—
> Father, Son, and Spirit together
> Chose to freely give

His Son—
> Chose
> That the second person of the Trinity
> Took human flesh
> Grew nine months in the womb
> Was birthed and thrived
> From infancy to toddlerhood
> From teens to manhood
> That he lived for 30 years or so
> In the vicinity
> Of 32 degrees North and 35 degrees East
> Under the vicissitudes of Roman rule

Trod the dusty roads of Palestine
Healing and teaching

God so loved the world
That he gave his only Son—
  To lay down his life to pay the price
  For sinful man to live again at peace with God

That whoever believes in him—
  Whoever believes
  From all that seething human mass
  Whoever looks on the face of the Son
  And trusts the love of Jesus and his hard work
         on the cross
  Though his body die his soul will live

That whoever believes in him
Will not perish
But have everlasting life.

Jesus Loves You

...unbending sources assure me that:
*   God is Good*
*   Jesus Loves Me*
*   and my Karma*
*   will be better next time...*
*   —— Randall Cadman ***

I long to strip the triteness
Out of "Jesus loves you"
Capture for your heart and mind
The sweep of story
Encompassed in that phrase

Unleash the words
From their over-familiarity
Wrest them
From the smug triviality you think you hear

The Creator of the Universe
Has walked the world for you
Accepted the indignity
Of your unreliable clay
Honored the glories
Of your everlasting soul
Spoken both tenderness and anger
Died, in pain and desolation
He took flesh's parentage
Lived as son and neighbor

          in a dusty Hebrew town
Went to a wedding
         and perhaps a funeral or two
Before his time came
To heal the sick and raise the dead

Before he bore his own rough wood
And all men's sin
Up the Hill of the Skull
Stretched out his arms
And died
For love of you

Then walked out of the tomb
And stretches his arms out still
For love of you.

For the Joy

Let us fix our eyes on Jesus...
who for the joy set before him
endured the cross.... (Hebrews 12:2)

Who for the joy set before him—
>   The joy of writing our names
>   in his book of life
>   Of clothing us with his righteousness
>   Of giving us a wedding garment
>   to wear to his feast

Who for the joy
>   Of making us new
>   Of exchanging our hearts of stone
>   For hearts of flesh

Who for the joy
>   Of sending us out with the glad news of
>   his coming
>   The glad news of sins forgiven
>   The glad news of life
>   abundant and unending

Who for the joy
Endured the cross.

He will see the result of the suffering of
his soul and be satisfied.
(Isaiah 53:11)*

Martha, When Lazarus Wasn't Dead Anymore

A Retelling of John 11

My brother was dead.
The breath had gone out of him,
All light from his eyes.
My brother Lazarus was dead.

That this should happen to us—
Us, who were so close to the healer,
The one whose very word or touch
Drove out illness, healed shrunken limbs!

We sent him word,
But he didn't come,
And Lazarus grew worse—
And then he was dead,
The breath and light all gone.

We did for him
What you do for the dead—
The washing and wrapping—
And then we placed his body in a tomb
And went away
And wept.

When Jesus finally came,
The first words out of my mouth

Were reproach—
"Lord, if you had been here,
My brother would not have died."   John 11:21

I did not understand,
When he replied to me,
That in a moment I would see him
Crack death wide open.

"I am the resurrection and the life."   John 11:25
His question was blunt,
"Do you believe this?"   John 11:26

I stammered.
"I believe you are Messiah."   John 11:27

He sent me to fetch Mary,
And when we returned
Jesus asked where we had laid him.
So we took him to the tomb.

Then he asked us to do an unthinkable thing—
He wanted us to move the stone
From the tomb of a man four days dead.

I knew what would come of that,
And I protested,
But once again his voice was compelling—
"Didn't I tell you that if you believed,
You would see the glory of God?"   John 11:40

So we rolled back the stone.
And Jesus shouted—
He shouted—
"Lazarus, come out!"   John 11:43

And Lazarus came out—
Death cracked wide open.

My brother was dead—

And tonight, I hear him in the next room,
talking.

So Much To Think About

But Mary treasured up all these things,
and pondered them in her heart. (Luke 2:19)

There was so much to think about
being his mother

From the very beginning
when the angel startled me with the announcement

So many questions—
What would Joseph think?
Would he believe me?
And my parents—

I was startled by Elizabeth's response
when I went to visit her
"Blessed are you," she exclaimed   Luke 1:42
and then words seemed to spill out
of both of us

There was so much to think about
being his mother
and the memories just piled up

The trip to Bethlehem with Joseph
was so difficult
and giving birth so far from home

without familiar faces attending
was not what we had hoped for

There were the shepherds
awkward and not altogether coherent
I had no problem believing their account of
angels
Angels were surrounding this child's birth

And the men from the East who visited later
with talk of a star
and the rich gifts they left behind
which served us well

I remember when we took him to the temple
for the dedication
We were scarcely in the gate
when Simeon and Anna were there
They were listening so closely
to the nudging of God
that they found us in a heartbeat

I'll never forget the looks on their faces
as they took the child from my arms
Those aged countenances glowed with the joy of hope fulfilled
Simeon's words engraved themselves in my mind
"A sword will pierce your own soul also."   Luke 2:35
They raised a pang of fear
and fear came again through the years
when I thought of them

When Joseph said to me,
there in Bethlehem,
"We must go now,"
and off we went
in the middle of the night
telling no one our destination
I wondered if this was one prick of that sword

And when we couldn't find him
after the trip to Jerusalem when he was twelve
We had walked a whole day toward home
and back we walked again to Jerusalem
and hunted everywhere for him
Finally we found him in the temple
He wasn't defiant
just patient, as if we should have understood

And there were joys—
the little things he did around the house
as he grew
the little easings and provisions
that showed he had authority over the things of earth
The way he treated the other children
and Joseph and me

A sword pierced my soul
when he left home
and began to travel about preaching
His brothers and I went one day
when we had learned what town he was in

It was crowded in the house
and we sent word in that we wanted to talk to him
His response trickled out to us
He had pointed to his disciples
and said, "Here are my mother and my brothers."   Matthew 12:49
Things were changing between us

And oh, the sword, the agony
the day he was crucified
I wanted to stay away
but how could I?
I was bewildered
How did this fit
with what the angel had said?
How did this fit
with an everlasting kingdom?

Those who had followed him
we who loved him
clung to each other
those next dark days
crushed by grief
hope flickering low

    And then the incredible

I had seen the lifeless body of my son
and now the tomb was empty
and angels again as at the beginning
"Why do you look for the living
among the dead?"   Luke 24:5

He appeared to various ones of us
to be seen
to be touched
and we waited together in Jerusalem
after he returned to Heaven

I experienced the wonders of Pentecost
and now here I stand
to worship and proclaim

"My Son, my Savior!"

Easter Laughter

Satan laughed
as they lowered the body
from the cross.

His rasping chortle
dogged every footstep to the tomb;
his mocking stabbed at every tear.
He laughed
from Friday to Sunday,
his glee unconstrained—

But then the earth shook;
the graveclothes lay empty,
the stone rolled back.
The crucified one stepped forth
in flesh that could not see death again,

And Jesus laughed,
his mouth wide, head flung back.
His joy pealed across the universe,
echoing from galaxy to galaxy—
wholesome, pure, triumphant—
the pain endured,
the battle finished,
his delight now unconstrained.

The risen Lord laughed,
he laughs,
and Satan weeps.

Thou hast kept count of my tossings;
    Put thou my tears in thy bottle!
    Are they not in thy book?
               Psalms 56:8 (RSV)

Cross Cure

Here at your feet
we tumble this basket
of brokenness,
this chaos of hearts crushed and bleeding,
of bodies aching and lame.

Sin takes its heavy toll
and leaves us speechless—
we have no defense.
Healer, Redeemer,
we are helpless.
There is no cure but blood and nails.

Make us whole, we plead,
and touch our wounds
with balm.

Body of Christ

All of you together are Christ's body, and each
of you is a part of it. (I Cor. 12:27) NLT

Spirit of God
courses through capillaries
sets nerves tingling
wakens the body

Eyes see deep lines of pain
in a suffering face
Ears listen
to a voice weary with discouragement

Skin to skin
hands cup another's cheek
in tenderness
wipe away tears

Lips speak words of hope
You are not alone
Emmanuel
God with us

Arms reach
to balance halting steps
We limp
We stumble

But finally Body will be Bride
and we shall dance.

In this World

"In this world, you will have trouble."

(John 16:33)

We don't understand

Through our tears
And broken hearts
We try to make sense of it all

And we don't understand

But you told us it would be so
And you said you told us
So we may have peace

And you told us too,
"Be of good cheer—
I have overcome the world."   John 16:33 RSV

So through our tears
And past our broken hearts
We choose again to trust You
And choose again
To be of good cheer

When we don't understand.

The God Without Pride

(a found poem) *

Part of my problem
　　With believing God loves me—

I wouldn't love me
　　Flighty,
　　Weak-willed,
　　Greedy for attention
These traits usually stay hidden,
Mask of humility in place.

I can't imagine being in love
With someone who didn't love me back—
　　I have my pride, after all.

Jesus stepped down to love—
　　Didn't he have any pride?

He doesn't need it.
He who makes the earth his footstool
　　Could hardly elevate himself further.

But love me?

Christ emptied himself—
　　I can't—not yet.

Christ emptied himself—
    I can't—not yet.

Can I surrender?
    Believe this heedless,
    Extravagant love for such as I?

His love
    Wild crystal stream
    Will tear away the last scrap of my unbelief—

From it I will emerge
    As free of pride as God himself.

        Found poem, based on "The God
        Without Pride,"
        Janie B. Cheaney, *World*,
        December 31, 2011

When You are Kissed by the King

(a found poem) *

Longing filled her heart—
If you were really beautiful
It was easy to be kind.

But what if you were just ordinary?
Life was not so easy then.
If you were nothing more than an ugly beggar,
Life was not so easy then.

The King himself
Has something to say to you—
All the subjects of the King are ugly beggars.
All the subjects of the King want to be as beautiful as he.

The King has something to say to you—
Go through the flames with me;
Be my guest at the banquet table.

The King has something to say to you—
When you are kissed by the King,
Your face is beautiful.

> A Found Poem
> from "The Girl Named Dirty,"
> *Tales of the Kingdom*,
> David and Karen Mains

Confession

And thou couldst see me sinning;
> —*Gerard Manley Hopkins* *

When you stretched out your arms and died,
You saw the days
When with barren heart
I have looked the other way
From suffering.

You saw the greedy grasping
Of what I thought I needed for myself
When I could have done another good.

You heard the harsh and unkind word,
Knew that I would not be
In love with truth
When it pointed to a path
That I found hard.

You knew the half-truths and omissions
For what they were—
You could see me sinning—
And yet,
And yet,
You stretched out your arms and died.

I bow, O Lord who sees me sinning,
And give you thanks!

Confession II

How leaden-footed I am,
How slow in coming to your throne
And asking
To see my sin.
That is a package
I would rather not unwrap.

But how gentle you are.
You have never forced that package upon me.
You have waited patiently for me to see
The need—
To creep into your presence and ask,
"Show me my sin."

My heart begged for gentleness,
And you are gentle—
But still I weep at what I see.
The messy layers peel back,
And there is so much left undone—
Discipline discarded,
Tasks trampled in the dust,
Whispered directions gone unheeded.

Oh, God of mercy,
Have mercy upon me.
Wash clean,
Build anew,
Create in me a heart
That obeys.

Propped Up

Propped up
>> leaning hard
>> on the goodness of God

Leaning
>> on this tower
>> that does not crumble

Leaning
>> on this one who does not waver

Propped up.

Smoldering Wicks

Our wicks are smoldering
nearly drowned in puddled oil
Tendrils of smoke
rise blackly with their dying

But you have said,
O God,
a smoldering wick
you will not snuff out

Blow on us,
sweet breath of Spirit,
that we may burn
with clear and lovely flame.

Communion Meditation

The bread and wine
Are in my hands

And I see the limbs
Nailed bleeding to the cross
Then raised in glory
Wounds still visible

I recognize the body, Lord,
Yours given for me
Paying the debt
That I cannot

And here is your body too
These dear flawed people
Whose debt is also paid
Who pass the plate
And wait
For bread and wine upon the tongue

Mysteriously
You weave your body
Those here and now
Sinew, blood, and cells
With those who have gone before
And with those who this day
Live and breathe a world away.

Martyred saints
Who bled and burned
All who suffer for the faith
And I, even I,
Are the body of Christ

Redeemed by your blood
Born of your spirit
We who are your body
Recognize your body, Lord,
And take here its sign
The bread and wine.

Fellowship of Forgiven Ones

Bound by the thread
Of the Master's mercy
We gather at his feet
In gladness and in hope

Admitted to his holy place
With all our pain
All our joy
Seeking his face

This fellowship of forgiven ones
Finding him in the Word spoken
And the Word written
And in one another's faces

We gather in gladness and in hope
This fellowship of forgiven ones
Bringing hearts of repentance and praise
Finding mercy at the foot of the cross.

"But the fruit of the Spirit is love, joy, peace, patience, kindness, goodness, faithfulness, gentleness and self-control. Against such things there is no law."

(Galatians 5:22-23)

Decorum

Then will the lame leap like a deer,
And the mute tongue shout for joy. (Isaiah 35:6)

For everyday wear, I don decorum—
Unobtrusive garb,
Disturbing no one
And when I want to dance
        around the sewing room
Shouting praise to God for turquoise velveteen,
No one is disturbed

When I yearn to skip along the water's edge
And clap my hands to startle a heron
Just to see his lovely, lumbering flight—
I take pity on the bird
And leave him in peace

Decorum would crack a bit
Should I surrender to the urge
To pick up a peacock feather from the ground
And wave it over my head all day long,
Raving at the glory of it!
Decorum would crack a bit,
Another eye and ear
Might find complacency disturbed

I keep waiting for the thund'rous day
When all decorum will be shattered,
All creation dance and skip and shout—
But that's too far away!
Today I want to uncage my heart,
Shout glory loudly enough for you to hear!
Shout glory!

For the Intercessors

Valiant Stretcher-Bearers,
who have carried the lame
on the cot of your prayers,
wrapped in kindness and care—
who have torn tiles off roofs
and lowered your friends
at the Master's feet,
cutting through the crowd and hurry
of your own days—

Persistent Petitioners,
who beg the Father's touch
in the dramas of our lives,
both small and great—
who murmur your brothers' and sisters' names
and walk the path with us
to steady our steps
through the rough places and trying times—

Strong Praying Saints,
your sinews strain
beneath the weight of this sin-sick world,
heaping it all at the foot of the cross,
pleading the healing blood
to give life to souls,
to open blind eyes,
to make bodies whole,
so all can leave the stretcher behind,
take up their beds and walk.

I Lean In

I lean in to you, O God
Sometimes in petition
Always in praise

You are the solidity
Undergirding every thought
Without you
There is nothing

I live my days
Aware of you
Turning to you
With the ease of breathing

Soil beneath my feet
Food in my mouth
Stir thankfulness to you,
Creator of all

And the gladness of redemption
Sin forgiven
Debts erased
At that terrible cross-cost

I lean in, O God
In awe and gratitude
Always in praise.

I Keep Asking

I keep asking that the God of our Lord Jesus Christ, the glorious
Father, may give you the Spirit of wisdom and revelation,
so that you may know him better. (Ephesians 1:17)

I keep asking—
>not casually
>nor only occasionally

I keep asking—
>often
>and with genuine desire

And whom do I ask?
>the glorious Father
>the One who is able
>to answer my prayer—
>the One who listens to his children
>who come in the name of Jesus

I keep asking
>that he will give you
>the spirit of wisdom

>of understanding and discernment
>>to make good choices
>>to choose the right path

the spirit of revelation
      that he will show you
      what is beyond the scope
      of your own mind

      that he will show you
         himself

so you may know him better

What better thing
than to know the Creator of the Universe
      Truly
      Clearly
      Intimately

So I keep asking
      For you
         And for myself.

Thanking God for Faithful Servants

Many faces
Will be before your throne, O Lord,
Because they told your story

Souls that were perishing
Found life
Because they held out a hand

Seeds of truth planted
Took root and flourished
Because they faithfully labored

Brothers and sisters
Have taken courage
Because of their courage

Our faces shine when we think of them,
Rejoicing with you, Lord,
Over these choice servants

And with them we praise you, our Father,
For the work your Spirit has done!

For Those Long Wed

To Guy and Marie
on the occasion of their 70th anniversary

When starry-eyed youth
Speak their vows
They cannot fathom growing old
Cannot grasp body's betrayal

But when marriage is measured in decades
When patience and forgiveness
Have been practiced
And practiced again

When "for better or worse"
Have both been tasted
When the promise
Has been kept year after year

We rejoice.

Infant

Here in my arms
lies Hope
whose present intent
is only to suckle and sleep
but whose fertile brain
is gathering sound and touch
whose eyes
are seeking to focus
beginning to recognize.

Here in my arms
lies Hope
latent discoveries and inventions
seeding from language
words finding meaning
in more than pitch and tone.
Nestled here
may Hope flourish
and outgrow my nurturing arms.

Death's Hard to Take

Whether it comes in sudden pounce
Or makes a long and visible approach,
Death's hard to take.
It stuns us, breaks our hearts,
Leaves us bereft of body's sweet tangibility,
Drives laughter and smiles out of reach.

But we are marked for saving,
Who look to the Lamb,
Who paint his blood on the doorposts
of our hearts.
Death seizes our feeble flesh,
But our souls are safe.

Here in the mercy of God we hide,
Sheltered and kept secure,
Passed over when judgment comes.

    Messiah, Messiah,
    I cling to your cross
    While the angel of death roars by!

Here

Here in this time
Now in this place
Secure that it is the right place
The right time
That you and I are not
Some cosmic blunder

Yet always a little uneasy in my own skin
Wondering
Were the choices I made the right ones?
Did I do the best I could?
What does God think?

Here in this time
Now in this place
Journeying
Not home yet
Even if it is the right time
The right place

Trusting that this meeting
Of time and place and self
Has purpose
Will end with meaning,
Not in emptiness.

Remembering

If his life
Had failed of its promise
We would remember nothing
Of angels
    shepherds
    and a natal star

The Jewish baby
Born in a barn
Would have no press today
If he had never fed the multitude
Or healed the blind
Or risen from the dead

But the manger-cradled child
Conquered sin and death
And will come again
King forevermore
And so we remember
    angels
    shepherds
    and a single Star.

Journey Home

To the cradle they came,
bowing before the Word made flesh.
Gifts they gave,
gold and frankincense and myrrh,
then outfoxed Herod,
going home another way.

We know the end of the story,
see him past the rough wood cradle,
see him on the rough wood cross,
see him risen from the tomb,
see him crowned with gold,
incense rising before him.

No need for hiding now
from jealous kings.
He is King himself,
and we bow
before manger, cross, and crown,
coming home the only way,
at last to stay.

Notes

Epigraph for "Desert Hymn": S.T. Coleridge, "Hymn Before Sunrise in the Vale of Chamouni."

Epigraph for "Jesus Loves You": Randall Cadman, "Another Reason to Have a Cat," from *Cat Fever*, handcrafted chapbook, inscribed by the author, 8/07.

Epigraph for "Confession": Gerard Manley Hopkins, "O Deus, ego amo te."

The translation of Isaiah 53:11 which appears with "For the Joy" is a footnote in the NIV Bible, from the Masoretic Text.

Psalms 56:8 stamp collage stamped by Rhonda Brown. Glass canning bottle: ©Good Stamps*Stamp Goods, artist Carole Finley, used by permission.
Madonna Image: Post Modern Design. Used by permission.

Pear: hand-carved image ©A Stamp in the Hand Co. Artist: Sue Nan Douglass. Stamped in watercolor marker by Rhonda Brown. Used by permission.

A found poem consists of words or phrases selected from the work of another author, which are then reordered to create a new poem. Both of the found poems in this collection are included here with the permission of the author of the original source material.

Found poem, "The God Without Pride," based on Janie B. Cheaney's piece by the same title, *World*, December 31, 2011.

Found Poem, "When You are Kissed by the King" from "The Girl Named Dirty," *Tales of the Kingdom*, David and Karen Mains.

The following poems have previously appeared in *Sandcutters*, the journal of the Arizona State Poetry Society:
"Ornament" — Summer 2008
"Desert Hymn" — Summer 2009
"Death's Hard to Take" — Autumn 2012
"Decorum" — Spring 2013

"Palo Verde" was published in *Arizona:100 Years, 100 Poems, 100 Poets,* 2012, edited by Stuart Watkins

Printed in the United States
by Baker & Taylor Publisher Services